THIS

GRANDAD'S CAMPING TRAVEL JOURNAL

BELONGS TO

Name ....

E MAIL ....

MOBILE ....

BLOG ....

PLEASE RETURN IF FOUND

CAMPING TRAVEL JOURNAL

DATE ..../..../.........   MILEAGE START ....

START TIME ....   MILEAGE END ....

ARRIVAL TIME ....   MILEAGE TOTAL ....

CAMPSITE NAME ....

ADDRESS 1 ....

ADDRESS 2 ....

POST CODE ....   GPS ....

E MAIL ....   PHONE ....

WEBSITE WWW..

MY RATING ☆☆☆☆☆☆☆☆☆☆   RECOMMEND YES/NO

WHAT 3 WORDS LOCATION ....

NUMBER OF NIGHTS HERE ....

PEOPLE WE MET - NAMES, E MAIL, PHONE NUMBER

....

....

....

....

DAILY COSTS		TODAY'S HIGHLIGHTS
SITE FEES	£	....
FUEL	£	....
LPG GAS	£	....
TOLLS	£	....
GROCERIES	£	....
EATING OUT	£	....
ENTERTAINMENT	£	....
OTHER COSTS	£	....

NOTES

....

....

....

....

....

CAMPING TRAVEL JOURNAL

DATE ..../..../.........   MILEAGE START ....

START TIME ....   MILEAGE END ....

ARRIVAL TIME ....   MILEAGE TOTAL ....

CAMPSITE NAME ....

ADDRESS I ....

ADDRESS 2 ....

POST CODE ....   GPS ....

E MAIL ....   PHONE ....

WEBSITE WWW...

MY RATING ☆☆☆☆☆☆☆☆☆☆   RECOMMEND YES/NO

WHAT 3 WORDS LOCATION ....

NUMBER OF NIGHTS HERE ....

PEOPLE WE MET - NAMES, E MAIL, PHONE NUMBER

....

....

....

....

DAILY COSTS

			TODAY'S HIGHLIGHTS
SITE FEES	£	....	....
FUEL	£	....	....
LPG GAS	£	....	....
TOLLS	£	....	....
GROCERIES	£	....	....
EATING OUT	£	....	....
ENTERTAINMENT	£	....	....
OTHER COSTS	£	....	....

NOTES

....

....

....

....

....

CAMPING TRAVEL JOURNAL

DATE ..../..../........ MILEAGE START ....

START TIME .... MILEAGE END ....

ARRIVAL TIME .... MILEAGE TOTAL ....

CAMPSITE NAME ....

ADDRESS 1 ....

ADDRESS 2 ....

POST CODE .... GPS ....

E MAIL .... PHONE ....

WEBSITE WWW..

MY RATING ☆☆☆☆☆☆☆☆☆☆ RECOMMEND YES/NO

WHAT 3 WORDS LOCATION ....

NUMBER OF NIGHTS HERE ....

PEOPLE WE MET - NAMES, E MAIL, PHONE NUMBER
....
....
....
....

DAILY COSTS		TODAY'S HIGHLIGHTS
SITE FEES	£	....
FUEL	£	....
LPG GAS	£	....
TOLLS	£	....
GROCERIES	£	....
EATING OUT	£	....
ENTERTAINMENT	£	....
OTHER COSTS	£	....

NOTES
....
....
....
....
....

CAMPING TRAVEL JOURNAL

DATE ..../..../.........   MILEAGE START ....

START TIME ....   MILEAGE END ....

ARRIVAL TIME ....   MILEAGE TOTAL ....

CAMPSITE NAME ....

ADDRESS 1 ....

ADDRESS 2 ....

POST CODE ....   GPS ....

E MAIL ....   PHONE ....

WEBSITE WWW...

MY RATING ☆☆☆☆☆☆☆☆☆☆   RECOMMEND YES/NO

WHAT 3 WORDS LOCATION ....

NUMBER OF NIGHTS HERE ....

PEOPLE WE MET - NAMES, E MAIL, PHONE NUMBER

....

....

....

....

DAILY COSTS		TODAY'S HIGHLIGHTS
SITE FEES	£	....
FUEL	£	....
LPG GAS	£	....
TOLLS	£	....
GROCERIES	£	....
EATING OUT	£	....
ENTERTAINMENT	£	....
OTHER COSTS	£	....

NOTES

....

....

....

....

....

CAMPING TRAVEL JOURNAL

DATE ..../..../......... MILEAGE START ....

START TIME .... MILEAGE END ....

ARRIVAL TIME .... MILEAGE TOTAL ....

CAMPSITE NAME ....

ADDRESS 1 ....

ADDRESS 2 ....

POST CODE .... GPS ....

E MAIL .... PHONE ....

WEBSITE WWW...

MY RATING ☆☆☆☆☆☆☆☆☆☆ RECOMMEND YES/NO

WHAT 3 WORDS LOCATION ....

NUMBER OF NIGHTS HERE ....

PEOPLE WE MET - NAMES, E MAIL, PHONE NUMBER
....
....
....
....

DAILY COSTS

		TODAY'S HIGHLIGHTS
SITE FEES	£	....
FUEL	£	....
LPG GAS	£	....
TOLLS	£	....
GROCERIES	£	....
EATING OUT	£	....
ENTERTAINMENT	£	....
OTHER COSTS	£	....

NOTES
....
....
....
....
....

CAMPING TRAVEL JOURNAL

DATE ..../..../......... MILEAGE START ....

START TIME .... MILEAGE END ....

ARRIVAL TIME .... MILEAGE TOTAL ....

CAMPSITE NAME ....

ADDRESS 1 ....

ADDRESS 2 ....

POST CODE .... GPS ....

E MAIL .... PHONE ....

WEBSITE WWW...

MY RATING ☆☆☆☆☆☆☆☆☆☆ RECOMMEND YES/NO

WHAT 3 WORDS LOCATION ....

NUMBER OF NIGHTS HERE ....

PEOPLE WE MET - NAMES, E MAIL, PHONE NUMBER

....

....

....

....

DAILY COSTS		TODAY'S HIGHLIGHTS
SITE FEES	£	....
FUEL	£	....
LPG GAS	£	....
TOLLS	£	....
GROCERIES	£	....
EATING OUT	£	....
ENTERTAINMENT	£	....
OTHER COSTS	£	....

NOTES

....

....

....

....

....

CAMPING TRAVEL JOURNAL

DATE ..../..../......... MILEAGE START ....

START TIME .... MILEAGE END ....

ARRIVAL TIME .... MILEAGE TOTAL ....

CAMPSITE NAME ....

ADDRESS 1 ....

ADDRESS 2 ....

POST CODE .... GPS ....

E MAIL .... PHONE ....

WEBSITE WWW...

MY RATING ☆☆☆☆☆☆☆☆☆☆ RECOMMEND YES/NO

WHAT 3 WORDS LOCATION ....

NUMBER OF NIGHTS HERE ....

PEOPLE WE MET - NAMES, E MAIL, PHONE NUMBER

....
....
....
....

DAILY COSTS		TODAY'S HIGHLIGHTS
SITE FEES	£	....
FUEL	£	....
LPG GAS	£	....
TOLLS	£	....
GROCERIES	£	....
EATING OUT	£	....
ENTERTAINMENT	£	....
OTHER COSTS	£	....

NOTES

....
....
....
....
....

CAMPING TRAVEL JOURNAL

DATE   ..../..../.........   MILEAGE START ....

START TIME   ....   MILEAGE END   ....

ARRIVAL TIME ....   MILEAGE TOTAL ....

CAMPSITE NAME ....

ADDRESS I ....

ADDRESS 2 ....

POST CODE ....   GPS ....

E MAIL ....   PHONE ....

WEBSITE WWW..

MY RATING ☆☆☆☆☆☆☆☆☆☆   RECOMMEND YES/NO

WHAT 3 WORDS LOCATION ....

NUMBER OF NIGHTS HERE ....

PEOPLE WE MET - NAMES, E MAIL, PHONE NUMBER

....
....
....
....

DAILY COSTS		TODAY'S HIGHLIGHTS
SITE FEES	£	....
FUEL	£	....
LPG GAS	£	....
TOLLS	£	....
GROCERIES	£	....
EATING OUT	£	....
ENTERTAINMENT	£	....
OTHER COSTS	£	....

NOTES

....
....
....
....
....

CAMPING TRAVEL JOURNAL

DATE ..../..../........ MILEAGE START ....

START TIME .... MILEAGE END ....

ARRIVAL TIME .... MILEAGE TOTAL ....

CAMPSITE NAME ....

ADDRESS 1 ....

ADDRESS 2 ....

POST CODE .... GPS ....

E MAIL .... PHONE ....

WEBSITE WWW..

MY RATING ☆☆☆☆☆☆☆☆☆☆ RECOMMEND YES/NO

WHAT 3 WORDS LOCATION ....

NUMBER OF NIGHTS HERE ....

PEOPLE WE MET - NAMES, E MAIL, PHONE NUMBER

....
....
....
....

DAILY COSTS		TODAY'S HIGHLIGHTS
SITE FEES	£	....
FUEL	£	....
LPG GAS	£	....
TOLLS	£	....
GROCERIES	£	....
EATING OUT	£	....
ENTERTAINMENT	£	....
OTHER COSTS	£	....

NOTES

....
....
....
....
....

CAMPING TRAVEL JOURNAL

DATE ..../..../......... MILEAGE START ....

START TIME .... MILEAGE END ....

ARRIVAL TIME .... MILEAGE TOTAL ....

CAMPSITE NAME ....

ADDRESS 1 ....

ADDRESS 2 ....

POST CODE .... GPS ....

E MAIL .... PHONE ....

WEBSITE WWW..

MY RATING ☆☆☆☆☆☆☆☆☆☆ RECOMMEND YES/NO

WHAT 3 WORDS LOCATION ....

NUMBER OF NIGHTS HERE ....

PEOPLE WE MET - NAMES, E MAIL, PHONE NUMBER

....

....

....

....

DAILY COSTS

		TODAY'S HIGHLIGHTS
SITE FEES	£	....
FUEL	£	....
LPG GAS	£	....
TOLLS	£	....
GROCERIES	£	....
EATING OUT	£	....
ENTERTAINMENT	£	....
OTHER COSTS	£	....

NOTES

....

....

....

....

....

CAMPING TRAVEL JOURNAL

DATE   ..../..../.........   MILEAGE START ....

START TIME ....   MILEAGE END   ....

ARRIVAL TIME ....   MILEAGE TOTAL ....

CAMPSITE NAME ....

ADDRESS 1 ....

ADDRESS 2 ....

POST CODE ....   GPS ....

E MAIL ....   PHONE ....

WEBSITE WWW...

MY RATING ☆☆☆☆☆☆☆☆☆☆   RECOMMEND YES/NO

WHAT 3 WORDS LOCATION ....

NUMBER OF NIGHTS HERE ....

PEOPLE WE MET - NAMES, E MAIL, PHONE NUMBER

....

....

....

....

DAILY COSTS		TODAY'S HIGHLIGHTS
SITE FEES	£	....
FUEL	£	....
LPG GAS	£	....
TOLLS	£	....
GROCERIES	£	....
EATING OUT	£	....
ENTERTAINMENT	£	....
OTHER COSTS	£	....

NOTES

....

....

....

....

....

CAMPING TRAVEL JOURNAL

DATE ..../..../......... MILEAGE START ....

START TIME .... MILEAGE END ....

ARRIVAL TIME .... MILEAGE TOTAL ....

CAMPSITE NAME ....

ADDRESS 1 ....

ADDRESS 2 ....

POST CODE .... GPS ....

E MAIL .... PHONE ....

WEBSITE WWW...

MY RATING ☆☆☆☆☆☆☆☆☆☆ RECOMMEND YES/NO

WHAT 3 WORDS LOCATION ....

NUMBER OF NIGHTS HERE ....

PEOPLE WE MET - NAMES, E MAIL, PHONE NUMBER

....

....

....

....

DAILY COSTS		TODAY'S HIGHLIGHTS
SITE FEES	£	....
FUEL	£	....
LPG GAS	£	....
TOLLS	£	....
GROCERIES	£	....
EATING OUT	£	....
ENTERTAINMENT	£	....
OTHER COSTS	£	....

NOTES

....

....

....

....

....

CAMPING TRAVEL JOURNAL

DATE   ..../..../.........   MILEAGE START ....

START TIME   ....   MILEAGE END   ....

ARRIVAL TIME ....   MILEAGE TOTAL ....

CAMPSITE NAME ....

ADDRESS 1 ....

ADDRESS 2 ....

POST CODE ....   GPS ....

E MAIL ....   PHONE ....

WEBSITE WWW...

MY RATING ☆☆☆☆☆☆☆☆☆☆   RECOMMEND YES/NO

WHAT 3 WORDS LOCATION ....

NUMBER OF NIGHTS HERE ....

PEOPLE WE MET - NAMES, E MAIL, PHONE NUMBER

....

....

....

....

DAILY COSTS		TODAY'S HIGHLIGHTS
SITE FEES	£	....
FUEL	£	....
LPG GAS	£	....
TOLLS	£	....
GROCERIES	£	....
EATING OUT	£	....
ENTERTAINMENT	£	....
OTHER COSTS	£	....

NOTES

....

....

....

....

....

CAMPING TRAVEL JOURNAL

DATE ..../..../......... MILEAGE START ....

START TIME .... MILEAGE END ....

ARRIVAL TIME .... MILEAGE TOTAL ....

CAMPSITE NAME ....

ADDRESS I ....

ADDRESS 2 ....

POST CODE .... GPS ....

E MAIL .... PHONE ....

WEBSITE WWW...

MY RATING ☆☆☆☆☆☆☆☆☆☆ RECOMMEND YES/NO

WHAT 3 WORDS LOCATION ....

NUMBER OF NIGHTS HERE ....

PEOPLE WE MET - NAMES, E MAIL, PHONE NUMBER

....

....

....

....

DAILY COSTS			TODAY'S HIGHLIGHTS
SITE FEES	£	....	....
FUEL	£	....	....
LPG GAS	£	....	....
TOLLS	£	....	....
GROCERIES	£	....	....
EATING OUT	£	....	....
ENTERTAINMENT	£	....	....
OTHER COSTS	£	....	....

NOTES

....

....

....

....

....

CAMPING TRAVEL JOURNAL

DATE ..../..../........ MILEAGE START ....

START TIME .... MILEAGE END ....

ARRIVAL TIME .... MILEAGE TOTAL ....

CAMPSITE NAME ....

ADDRESS 1 ....

ADDRESS 2 ....

POST CODE .... GPS ....

E MAIL .... PHONE ....

WEBSITE WWW..

MY RATING ☆☆☆☆☆☆☆☆☆☆ RECOMMEND YES/NO

WHAT 3 WORDS LOCATION ....

NUMBER OF NIGHTS HERE ....

PEOPLE WE MET - NAMES, E MAIL, PHONE NUMBER

....

....

....

....

DAILY COSTS		TODAY'S HIGHLIGHTS
SITE FEES	£	....
FUEL	£	....
LPG GAS	£	....
TOLLS	£	....
GROCERIES	£	....
EATING OUT	£	....
ENTERTAINMENT	£	....
OTHER COSTS	£	....

NOTES

....

....

....

....

....

CAMPING TRAVEL JOURNAL

DATE ..../..../.........   MILEAGE START ....

START TIME ....   MILEAGE END ....

ARRIVAL TIME ....   MILEAGE TOTAL ....

CAMPSITE NAME ....

ADDRESS 1 ....

ADDRESS 2 ....

POST CODE ....   GPS ....

E MAIL ....   PHONE ....

WEBSITE WWW..

MY RATING ☆☆☆☆☆☆☆☆☆☆   RECOMMEND YES/NO

WHAT 3 WORDS LOCATION ....

NUMBER OF NIGHTS HERE ....

PEOPLE WE MET - NAMES, E MAIL, PHONE NUMBER

....
....
....
....

DAILY COSTS		TODAY'S HIGHLIGHTS
SITE FEES	£	....
FUEL	£	....
LPG GAS	£	....
TOLLS	£	....
GROCERIES	£	....
EATING OUT	£	....
ENTERTAINMENT	£	....
OTHER COSTS	£	....

NOTES

....
....
....
....
....

CAMPING TRAVEL JOURNAL

DATE .…/.…/……… MILEAGE START …………………

START TIME ……………… MILEAGE END ………………………

ARRIVAL TIME ……………… MILEAGE TOTAL …………………

CAMPSITE NAME ……………………………………………

ADDRESS 1 ………………………………………………………

ADDRESS 2 ………………………………………………………

POST CODE …………………… GPS …………………………………

E MAIL ……………………………… PHONE ………………………………

WEBSITE WWW……………………………………………………

MY RATING ☆☆☆☆☆☆☆☆☆☆ RECOMMEND YES/NO

WHAT 3 WORDS LOCATION ………………………………………

NUMBER OF NIGHTS HERE ……

PEOPLE WE MET - NAMES, E MAIL, PHONE NUMBER

……………………………………………………………………

……………………………………………………………………

……………………………………………………………………

……………………………………………………………………

DAILY COSTS		TODAY'S HIGHLIGHTS
SITE FEES	£ …………………	………………………………………
FUEL	£ …………………	………………………………………
LPG GAS	£ …………………	………………………………………
TOLLS	£ …………………	………………………………………
GROCERIES	£ …………………	………………………………………
EATING OUT	£ …………………	………………………………………
ENTERTAINMENT	£ …………………	………………………………………
OTHER COSTS	£ …………………	………………………………………

NOTES

……………………………………………………………………

……………………………………………………………………

……………………………………………………………………

……………………………………………………………………

……………………………………………………………………

CAMPING TRAVEL JOURNAL

DATE ..../..../......... MILEAGE START ....

START TIME .... MILEAGE END ....

ARRIVAL TIME .... MILEAGE TOTAL ....

CAMPSITE NAME ....

ADDRESS 1 ....

ADDRESS 2 ....

POST CODE .... GPS ....

E MAIL .... PHONE ....

WEBSITE WWW...

MY RATING ☆☆☆☆☆☆☆☆☆☆ RECOMMEND YES/NO

WHAT 3 WORDS LOCATION ....

NUMBER OF NIGHTS HERE ....

PEOPLE WE MET - NAMES, E MAIL, PHONE NUMBER

....

....

....

....

DAILY COSTS		TODAY'S HIGHLIGHTS
SITE FEES	£	....
FUEL	£	....
LPG GAS	£	....
TOLLS	£	....
GROCERIES	£	....
EATING OUT	£	....
ENTERTAINMENT	£	....
OTHER COSTS	£	....

NOTES

....

....

....

....

....

CAMPING TRAVEL JOURNAL

DATE ..../..../......... MILEAGE START ....

START TIME .... MILEAGE END ....

ARRIVAL TIME .... MILEAGE TOTAL ....

CAMPSITE NAME ....

ADDRESS 1 ....

ADDRESS 2 ....

POST CODE .... GPS ....

E MAIL .... PHONE ....

WEBSITE WWW...

MY RATING ☆☆☆☆☆☆☆☆☆☆ RECOMMEND YES/NO

WHAT 3 WORDS LOCATION ....

NUMBER OF NIGHTS HERE ....

PEOPLE WE MET - NAMES, E MAIL, PHONE NUMBER

....

....

....

....

DAILY COSTS

SITE FEES	£	....
FUEL	£	....
LPG GAS	£	....
TOLLS	£	....
GROCERIES	£	....
EATING OUT	£	....
ENTERTAINMENT	£	....
OTHER COSTS	£	....

TODAY'S HIGHLIGHTS

....

....

....

....

....

....

....

NOTES

....

....

....

....

....

CAMPING TRAVEL JOURNAL

DATE   ..../..../......... MILEAGE START ....
START TIME .... MILEAGE END ....
ARRIVAL TIME .... MILEAGE TOTAL ....

CAMPSITE NAME ....
ADDRESS I ....
ADDRESS 2 ....
POST CODE .... GPS ....
E MAIL .... PHONE ....
WEBSITE WWW...
MY RATING ☆☆☆☆☆☆☆☆☆☆   RECOMMEND YES/NO
WHAT 3 WORDS LOCATION ....
NUMBER OF NIGHTS HERE ....

PEOPLE WE MET - NAMES, E MAIL, PHONE NUMBER
....
....
....
....

DAILY COSTS		TODAY'S HIGHLIGHTS
SITE FEES	£	....
FUEL	£	....
LPG GAS	£	....
TOLLS	£	....
GROCERIES	£	....
EATING OUT	£	....
ENTERTAINMENT	£	....
OTHER COSTS	£	....

NOTES
....
....
....
....
....

CAMPING TRAVEL JOURNAL

DATE ..../..../........   MILEAGE START ....

START TIME .... MILEAGE END ....

ARRIVAL TIME .... MILEAGE TOTAL ....

CAMPSITE NAME ....

ADDRESS 1 ....

ADDRESS 2 ....

POST CODE ....   GPS ....

E MAIL ....   PHONE ....

WEBSITE WWW...

MY RATING ☆☆☆☆☆☆☆☆☆☆   RECOMMEND YES/NO

WHAT 3 WORDS LOCATION ....

NUMBER OF NIGHTS HERE ....

PEOPLE WE MET - NAMES, E MAIL, PHONE NUMBER

....
....
....
....

DAILY COSTS		TODAY'S HIGHLIGHTS
SITE FEES	£	....
FUEL	£	....
LPG GAS	£	....
TOLLS	£	....
GROCERIES	£	....
EATING OUT	£	....
ENTERTAINMENT	£	....
OTHER COSTS	£	....

NOTES

....
....
....
....
....

CAMPING TRAVEL JOURNAL

DATE ..../..../......... MILEAGE START ....

START TIME .... MILEAGE END ....

ARRIVAL TIME .... MILEAGE TOTAL ....

CAMPSITE NAME ....

ADDRESS I ....

ADDRESS 2 ....

POST CODE .... GPS ....

E MAIL .... PHONE ....

WEBSITE WWW..

MY RATING ☆☆☆☆☆☆☆☆☆☆ RECOMMEND YES/NO

WHAT 3 WORDS LOCATION ....

NUMBER OF NIGHTS HERE ....

PEOPLE WE MET - NAMES, E MAIL, PHONE NUMBER

....

....

....

....

DAILY COSTS		TODAY'S HIGHLIGHTS
SITE FEES	£	....
FUEL	£	....
LPG GAS	£	....
TOLLS	£	....
GROCERIES	£	....
EATING OUT	£	....
ENTERTAINMENT	£	....
OTHER COSTS	£	....

NOTES

....

....

....

....

....

CAMPING TRAVEL JOURNAL

DATE ..../..../......... MILEAGE START ....

START TIME .... MILEAGE END ....

ARRIVAL TIME .... MILEAGE TOTAL ....

CAMPSITE NAME ....

ADDRESS 1 ....

ADDRESS 2 ....

POST CODE .... GPS ....

E MAIL .... PHONE ....

WEBSITE WWW..

MY RATING ☆☆☆☆☆☆☆☆☆☆ RECOMMEND YES/NO

WHAT 3 WORDS LOCATION ....

NUMBER OF NIGHTS HERE ....

PEOPLE WE MET - NAMES, E MAIL, PHONE NUMBER

....

....

....

....

DAILY COSTS		TODAY'S HIGHLIGHTS
SITE FEES	£	....
FUEL	£	....
LPG GAS	£	....
TOLLS	£	....
GROCERIES	£	....
EATING OUT	£	....
ENTERTAINMENT	£	....
OTHER COSTS	£	....

NOTES

....

....

....

....

....

CAMPING TRAVEL JOURNAL

DATE ..../..../......... MILEAGE START ....

START TIME .... MILEAGE END ....

ARRIVAL TIME .... MILEAGE TOTAL ....

CAMPSITE NAME ....

ADDRESS I ....

ADDRESS 2 ....

POST CODE .... GPS ....

E MAIL .... PHONE ....

WEBSITE WWW...

MY RATING ☆☆☆☆☆☆☆☆☆☆ RECOMMEND YES/NO

WHAT 3 WORDS LOCATION ....

NUMBER OF NIGHTS HERE ....

PEOPLE WE MET - NAMES, E MAIL, PHONE NUMBER

....

....

....

....

DAILY COSTS	TODAY'S HIGHLIGHTS
SITE FEES £	....
FUEL £	....
LPG GAS £	....
TOLLS £	....
GROCERIES £	....
EATING OUT £	....
ENTERTAINMENT £	....
OTHER COSTS £	....

NOTES

....

....

....

....

....

CAMPING TRAVEL JOURNAL

DATE ..../..../......... MILEAGE START ....

START TIME .... MILEAGE END ....

ARRIVAL TIME .... MILEAGE TOTAL ....

CAMPSITE NAME ....

ADDRESS 1 ....

ADDRESS 2 ....

POST CODE .... GPS ....

E MAIL .... PHONE ....

WEBSITE WWW...

MY RATING ☆☆☆☆☆☆☆☆☆☆ RECOMMEND YES/NO

WHAT 3 WORDS LOCATION ....

NUMBER OF NIGHTS HERE ....

PEOPLE WE MET - NAMES, E MAIL, PHONE NUMBER

....
....
....
....

DAILY COSTS		TODAY'S HIGHLIGHTS
SITE FEES	£	....
FUEL	£	....
LPG GAS	£	....
TOLLS	£	....
GROCERIES	£	....
EATING OUT	£	....
ENTERTAINMENT	£	....
OTHER COSTS	£	....

NOTES

....
....
....
....
....

CAMPING TRAVEL JOURNAL

DATE ..../..../......... MILEAGE START ....

START TIME .... MILEAGE END ....

ARRIVAL TIME .... MILEAGE TOTAL ....

CAMPSITE NAME ....

ADDRESS 1 ....

ADDRESS 2 ....

POST CODE .... GPS ....

E MAIL .... PHONE ....

WEBSITE WWW...

MY RATING ☆☆☆☆☆☆☆☆☆☆ RECOMMEND YES/NO

WHAT 3 WORDS LOCATION ....

NUMBER OF NIGHTS HERE ....

PEOPLE WE MET - NAMES, E MAIL, PHONE NUMBER
....
....
....
....

DAILY COSTS		TODAY'S HIGHLIGHTS
SITE FEES	£	....
FUEL	£	....
LPG GAS	£	....
TOLLS	£	....
GROCERIES	£	....
EATING OUT	£	....
ENTERTAINMENT	£	....
OTHER COSTS	£	....

NOTES
....
....
....
....
....

CAMPING TRAVEL JOURNAL

DATE ..../..../.........   MILEAGE START ....

START TIME ....   MILEAGE END ....

ARRIVAL TIME ....   MILEAGE TOTAL ....

CAMPSITE NAME ....

ADDRESS 1 ....

ADDRESS 2 ....

POST CODE ....   GPS ....

E MAIL ....   PHONE ....

WEBSITE WWW..

MY RATING ☆☆☆☆☆☆☆☆☆☆   RECOMMEND YES/NO

WHAT 3 WORDS LOCATION ....

NUMBER OF NIGHTS HERE ....

PEOPLE WE MET - NAMES, E MAIL, PHONE NUMBER

....
....
....
....

DAILY COSTS		TODAY'S HIGHLIGHTS
SITE FEES	£	....
FUEL	£	....
LPG GAS	£	....
TOLLS	£	....
GROCERIES	£	....
EATING OUT	£	....
ENTERTAINMENT	£	....
OTHER COSTS	£	....

NOTES

....
....
....
....
....

CAMPING TRAVEL JOURNAL

DATE ...../...../......... MILEAGE START ....

START TIME .... MILEAGE END ....

ARRIVAL TIME .... MILEAGE TOTAL ....

CAMPSITE NAME ....

ADDRESS I ....

ADDRESS 2 ....

POST CODE .... GPS ....

E MAIL .... PHONE ....

WEBSITE WWW...

MY RATING ☆☆☆☆☆☆☆☆☆☆ RECOMMEND YES/NO

WHAT 3 WORDS LOCATION ....

NUMBER OF NIGHTS HERE ....

PEOPLE WE MET - NAMES, E MAIL, PHONE NUMBER

....
....
....
....

DAILY COSTS		TODAY'S HIGHLIGHTS
SITE FEES	£	....
FUEL	£	....
LPG GAS	£	....
TOLLS	£	....
GROCERIES	£	....
EATING OUT	£	....
ENTERTAINMENT	£	....
OTHER COSTS	£	....

NOTES

....
....
....
....
....

CAMPING TRAVEL JOURNAL

DATE ..../..../......... MILEAGE START ....

START TIME .... MILEAGE END ....

ARRIVAL TIME .... MILEAGE TOTAL ....

CAMPSITE NAME ....

ADDRESS 1 ....

ADDRESS 2 ....

POST CODE .... GPS ....

E MAIL .... PHONE ....

WEBSITE WWW..

MY RATING ☆☆☆☆☆☆☆☆☆☆ RECOMMEND YES/NO

WHAT 3 WORDS LOCATION ....

NUMBER OF NIGHTS HERE ....

PEOPLE WE MET - NAMES, E MAIL, PHONE NUMBER

....

....

....

....

DAILY COSTS

			TODAY'S HIGHLIGHTS
SITE FEES	£	....	....
FUEL	£	....	....
LPG GAS	£	....	....
TOLLS	£	....	....
GROCERIES	£	....	....
EATING OUT	£	....	....
ENTERTAINMENT	£	....	....
OTHER COSTS	£	....	....

NOTES

....

....

....

....

....

CAMPING TRAVEL JOURNAL

DATE ...../...../......... MILEAGE START ....

START TIME .... MILEAGE END ....

ARRIVAL TIME .... MILEAGE TOTAL ....

CAMPSITE NAME ....

ADDRESS 1 ....

ADDRESS 2 ....

POST CODE .... GPS ....

E MAIL .... PHONE ....

WEBSITE WWW..

MY RATING ☆☆☆☆☆☆☆☆☆☆ RECOMMEND YES/NO

WHAT 3 WORDS LOCATION ....

NUMBER OF NIGHTS HERE ....

PEOPLE WE MET - NAMES, E MAIL, PHONE NUMBER

....

....

....

....

DAILY COSTS		TODAY'S HIGHLIGHTS
SITE FEES	£	....
FUEL	£	....
LPG GAS	£	....
TOLLS	£	....
GROCERIES	£	....
EATING OUT	£	....
ENTERTAINMENT	£	....
OTHER COSTS	£	

NOTES

....

....

....

....

....

CAMPING TRAVEL JOURNAL

DATE ...../...../.........   MILEAGE START ....

START TIME ....   MILEAGE END ....

ARRIVAL TIME ....   MILEAGE TOTAL ....

CAMPSITE NAME ....

ADDRESS 1 ....

ADDRESS 2 ....

POST CODE ....   GPS ....

E MAIL ....   PHONE ....

WEBSITE WWW...

MY RATING ☆☆☆☆☆☆☆☆☆☆   RECOMMEND YES/NO

WHAT 3 WORDS LOCATION ....

NUMBER OF NIGHTS HERE ....

PEOPLE WE MET - NAMES, E MAIL, PHONE NUMBER

....
....
....
....

DAILY COSTS		TODAY'S HIGHLIGHTS
SITE FEES	£	....
FUEL	£	....
LPG GAS	£	....
TOLLS	£	....
GROCERIES	£	....
EATING OUT	£	....
ENTERTAINMENT	£	....
OTHER COSTS	£	....

NOTES

....
....
....
....
....

CAMPING TRAVEL JOURNAL

DATE ..../..../.........   MILEAGE START ....

START TIME ....   MILEAGE END ....

ARRIVAL TIME ....   MILEAGE TOTAL ....

CAMPSITE NAME ....

ADDRESS 1 ....

ADDRESS 2 ....

POST CODE ....   GPS ....

E MAIL ....   PHONE ....

WEBSITE WWW..

MY RATING ☆☆☆☆☆☆☆☆☆☆   RECOMMEND YES/NO

WHAT 3 WORDS LOCATION ....

NUMBER OF NIGHTS HERE ....

PEOPLE WE MET - NAMES, E MAIL, PHONE NUMBER

....
....
....
....

DAILY COSTS		TODAY'S HIGHLIGHTS
SITE FEES	£	....
FUEL	£	....
LPG GAS	£	....
TOLLS	£	....
GROCERIES	£	....
EATING OUT	£	....
ENTERTAINMENT	£	....
OTHER COSTS	£	....

NOTES

....
....
....
....
....

CAMPING TRAVEL JOURNAL

DATE   ..../..../.........   MILEAGE START ....

START TIME ....   MILEAGE END ....

ARRIVAL TIME ....   MILEAGE TOTAL ....

CAMPSITE NAME ....

ADDRESS 1 ....

ADDRESS 2 ....

POST CODE ....   GPS ....

E MAIL ....   PHONE ....

WEBSITE WWW..

MY RATING ☆☆☆☆☆☆☆☆☆☆   RECOMMEND YES/NO

WHAT 3 WORDS LOCATION ....

NUMBER OF NIGHTS HERE ....

PEOPLE WE MET - NAMES, E MAIL, PHONE NUMBER

....

....

....

....

DAILY COSTS		TODAY'S HIGHLIGHTS
SITE FEES	£	....
FUEL	£	....
LPG GAS	£	....
TOLLS	£	....
GROCERIES	£	....
EATING OUT	£	....
ENTERTAINMENT	£	....
OTHER COSTS	£	....

NOTES

....

....

....

....

....

CAMPING TRAVEL JOURNAL

DATE ..../..../.........   MILEAGE START ....

START TIME ....   MILEAGE END ....

ARRIVAL TIME ....   MILEAGE TOTAL ....

CAMPSITE NAME ....

ADDRESS I ....

ADDRESS 2 ....

POST CODE ....   GPS ....

E MAIL ....   PHONE ....

WEBSITE WWW..

MY RATING ☆ ☆ ☆ ☆ ☆ ☆ ☆ ☆ ☆ ☆   RECOMMEND YES/NO

WHAT 3 WORDS LOCATION ....

NUMBER OF NIGHTS HERE ....

PEOPLE WE MET - NAMES, E MAIL, PHONE NUMBER

....

....

....

....

DAILY COSTS		TODAY'S HIGHLIGHTS
SITE FEES	£	....
FUEL	£	....
LPG GAS	£	....
TOLLS	£	....
GROCERIES	£	....
EATING OUT	£	....
ENTERTAINMENT	£	....
OTHER COSTS	£	....

NOTES

....

....

....

....

....

CAMPING TRAVEL JOURNAL

DATE ..../..../......... MILEAGE START ....

START TIME .... MILEAGE END ....

ARRIVAL TIME .... MILEAGE TOTAL ....

CAMPSITE NAME ....

ADDRESS I ....

ADDRESS 2 ....

POST CODE .... GPS ....

E MAIL .... PHONE ....

WEBSITE WWW...

MY RATING ☆☆☆☆☆☆☆☆☆☆ RECOMMEND YES/NO

WHAT 3 WORDS LOCATION ....

NUMBER OF NIGHTS HERE ....

PEOPLE WE MET - NAMES, E MAIL, PHONE NUMBER

....
....
....
....

DAILY COSTS		TODAY'S HIGHLIGHTS
SITE FEES	£	....
FUEL	£	....
LPG GAS	£	....
TOLLS	£	....
GROCERIES	£	....
EATING OUT	£	....
ENTERTAINMENT	£	....
OTHER COSTS	£	....

NOTES

....
....
....
....
....

CAMPING TRAVEL JOURNAL

DATE ..../..../......... MILEAGE START ....

START TIME .... MILEAGE END ....

ARRIVAL TIME .... MILEAGE TOTAL ....

CAMPSITE NAME ....

ADDRESS 1 ....

ADDRESS 2 ....

POST CODE .... GPS ....

E MAIL .... PHONE ....

WEBSITE WWW...

MY RATING ☆☆☆☆☆☆☆☆☆☆ RECOMMEND YES/NO

WHAT 3 WORDS LOCATION ....

NUMBER OF NIGHTS HERE ....

PEOPLE WE MET - NAMES, E MAIL, PHONE NUMBER

....
....
....
....

DAILY COSTS		TODAY'S HIGHLIGHTS
SITE FEES	£	....
FUEL	£	....
LPG GAS	£	....
TOLLS	£	....
GROCERIES	£	....
EATING OUT	£	....
ENTERTAINMENT	£	....
OTHER COSTS	£	....

NOTES

....
....
....
....
....

CAMPING TRAVEL JOURNAL

DATE ..../..../......... MILEAGE START ....

START TIME .... MILEAGE END ....

ARRIVAL TIME .... MILEAGE TOTAL ....

CAMPSITE NAME ....

ADDRESS 1 ....

ADDRESS 2 ....

POST CODE .... GPS ....

E MAIL .... PHONE ....

WEBSITE WWW..

MY RATING ☆☆☆☆☆☆☆☆☆☆ RECOMMEND YES/NO

WHAT 3 WORDS LOCATION ....

NUMBER OF NIGHTS HERE ....

PEOPLE WE MET - NAMES, E MAIL, PHONE NUMBER

....

....

....

....

DAILY COSTS		TODAY'S HIGHLIGHTS
SITE FEES	£	....
FUEL	£	....
LPG GAS	£	....
TOLLS	£	....
GROCERIES	£	....
EATING OUT	£	....
ENTERTAINMENT	£	....
OTHER COSTS	£	....

NOTES

....

....

....

....

....

CAMPING TRAVEL JOURNAL

DATE ..../..../......... MILEAGE START ....

START TIME .... MILEAGE END ....

ARRIVAL TIME .... MILEAGE TOTAL ....

CAMPSITE NAME ....

ADDRESS I ....

ADDRESS 2 ....

POST CODE .... GPS ....

E MAIL .... PHONE ....

WEBSITE WWW..

MY RATING ☆☆☆☆☆☆☆☆☆☆ RECOMMEND YES/NO

WHAT 3 WORDS LOCATION ....

NUMBER OF NIGHTS HERE ....

PEOPLE WE MET - NAMES, E MAIL, PHONE NUMBER
....
....
....
....

DAILY COSTS		TODAY'S HIGHLIGHTS
SITE FEES	£	....
FUEL	£	....
LPG GAS	£	....
TOLLS	£	....
GROCERIES	£	....
EATING OUT	£	....
ENTERTAINMENT	£	....
OTHER COSTS	£	

NOTES

....

....

....

....

....

CAMPING TRAVEL JOURNAL

DATE ..../..../......... MILEAGE START ....

START TIME .... MILEAGE END ....

ARRIVAL TIME .... MILEAGE TOTAL ....

CAMPSITE NAME ....

ADDRESS 1 ....

ADDRESS 2 ....

POST CODE .... GPS ....

E MAIL .... PHONE ....

WEBSITE WWW...

MY RATING ☆☆☆☆☆☆☆☆☆ RECOMMEND YES/NO

WHAT 3 WORDS LOCATION ....

NUMBER OF NIGHTS HERE ....

PEOPLE WE MET - NAMES, E MAIL, PHONE NUMBER
....
....
....
....

DAILY COSTS

SITE FEES	£	....
FUEL	£	....
LPG GAS	£	....
TOLLS	£	....
GROCERIES	£	....
EATING OUT	£	....
ENTERTAINMENT	£	....
OTHER COSTS	£	....

TODAY'S HIGHLIGHTS
....
....
....
....
....
....
....

NOTES
....
....
....
....
....

CAMPING TRAVEL JOURNAL

DATE ..../..../......... MILEAGE START ....

START TIME .... MILEAGE END ....

ARRIVAL TIME .... MILEAGE TOTAL ....

CAMPSITE NAME ....

ADDRESS I ....

ADDRESS 2 ....

POST CODE .... GPS ....

E MAIL .... PHONE ....

WEBSITE WWW...

MY RATING ☆☆☆☆☆☆☆☆☆☆ RECOMMEND YES/NO

WHAT 3 WORDS LOCATION ....

NUMBER OF NIGHTS HERE ....

PEOPLE WE MET - NAMES, E MAIL, PHONE NUMBER
....
....
....
....

DAILY COSTS		TODAY'S HIGHLIGHTS
SITE FEES	£	....
FUEL	£	....
LPG GAS	£	....
TOLLS	£	....
GROCERIES	£	....
EATING OUT	£	....
ENTERTAINMENT	£	....
OTHER COSTS	£	....

NOTES
....
....
....
....
....

CAMPING TRAVEL JOURNAL

DATE ...../...../......... MILEAGE START ....

START TIME .... MILEAGE END ....

ARRIVAL TIME .... MILEAGE TOTAL ....

CAMPSITE NAME ....

ADDRESS 1 ....

ADDRESS 2 ....

POST CODE .... GPS ....

E MAIL .... PHONE ....

WEBSITE WWW..

MY RATING ☆☆☆☆☆☆☆☆☆☆ RECOMMEND YES/NO

WHAT 3 WORDS LOCATION ....

NUMBER OF NIGHTS HERE ....

PEOPLE WE MET - NAMES, E MAIL, PHONE NUMBER

....

....

....

....

DAILY COSTS		TODAY'S HIGHLIGHTS
SITE FEES	£	....
FUEL	£	....
LPG GAS	£	....
TOLLS	£	....
GROCERIES	£	....
EATING OUT	£	....
ENTERTAINMENT	£	....
OTHER COSTS	£	....

NOTES

....

....

....

....

....

CAMPING TRAVEL JOURNAL

DATE ..../..../......... MILEAGE START ....

START TIME .... MILEAGE END ....

ARRIVAL TIME .... MILEAGE TOTAL ....

CAMPSITE NAME ....

ADDRESS 1 ....

ADDRESS 2 ....

POST CODE .... GPS ....

E MAIL .... PHONE ....

WEBSITE WWW...

MY RATING ☆☆☆☆☆☆☆☆☆☆ RECOMMEND YES/NO

WHAT 3 WORDS LOCATION ....

NUMBER OF NIGHTS HERE ....

PEOPLE WE MET - NAMES, E MAIL, PHONE NUMBER

....

....

....

....

DAILY COSTS		TODAY'S HIGHLIGHTS
SITE FEES	£	....
FUEL	£	....
LPG GAS	£	....
TOLLS	£	....
GROCERIES	£	....
EATING OUT	£	....
ENTERTAINMENT	£	....
OTHER COSTS	£	....

NOTES

....

....

....

....

....

CAMPING TRAVEL JOURNAL

DATE ..../..../......... MILEAGE START ....

START TIME .... MILEAGE END ....

ARRIVAL TIME .... MILEAGE TOTAL ....

CAMPSITE NAME ....

ADDRESS 1 ....

ADDRESS 2 ....

POST CODE .... GPS ....

E MAIL .... PHONE ....

WEBSITE WWW..

MY RATING ☆☆☆☆☆☆☆☆☆☆ RECOMMEND YES/NO

WHAT 3 WORDS LOCATION ....

NUMBER OF NIGHTS HERE ....

PEOPLE WE MET - NAMES, E MAIL, PHONE NUMBER

....

....

....

....

DAILY COSTS	TODAY'S HIGHLIGHTS
SITE FEES £	....
FUEL £	....
LPG GAS £	....
TOLLS £	....
GROCERIES £	....
EATING OUT £	....
ENTERTAINMENT £	....
OTHER COSTS £	....

NOTES

....

....

....

....

....

CAMPING TRAVEL JOURNAL

DATE ..../..../......... MILEAGE START ....

START TIME .... MILEAGE END ....

ARRIVAL TIME .... MILEAGE TOTAL ....

CAMPSITE NAME ....

ADDRESS 1 ....

ADDRESS 2 ....

POST CODE .... GPS ....

E MAIL .... PHONE ....

WEBSITE WWW...

MY RATING ☆☆☆☆☆☆☆☆☆☆ RECOMMEND YES/NO

WHAT 3 WORDS LOCATION ....

NUMBER OF NIGHTS HERE ....

PEOPLE WE MET - NAMES, E MAIL, PHONE NUMBER

....

....

....

....

DAILY COSTS		TODAY'S HIGHLIGHTS
SITE FEES	£	....
FUEL	£	....
LPG GAS	£	....
TOLLS	£	....
GROCERIES	£	....
EATING OUT	£	....
ENTERTAINMENT	£	....
OTHER COSTS	£	....

NOTES

....

....

....

....

....

CAMPING TRAVEL JOURNAL

DATE ..../..../........ MILEAGE START ....

START TIME .... MILEAGE END ....

ARRIVAL TIME .... MILEAGE TOTAL ....

CAMPSITE NAME ....

ADDRESS I ....

ADDRESS 2 ....

POST CODE .... GPS ....

E MAIL .... PHONE ....

WEBSITE WWW..

MY RATING ☆☆☆☆☆☆☆☆☆☆ RECOMMEND YES/NO

WHAT 3 WORDS LOCATION ....

NUMBER OF NIGHTS HERE ....

PEOPLE WE MET - NAMES, E MAIL, PHONE NUMBER

....
....
....
....

DAILY COSTS		TODAY'S HIGHLIGHTS
SITE FEES	£	....
FUEL	£	....
LPG GAS	£	....
TOLLS	£	....
GROCERIES	£	....
EATING OUT	£	....
ENTERTAINMENT	£	....
OTHER COSTS	£	

NOTES

....
....
....
....
....

CAMPING TRAVEL JOURNAL

DATE ..../..../......... MILEAGE START ....

START TIME .... MILEAGE END ....

ARRIVAL TIME .... MILEAGE TOTAL ....

CAMPSITE NAME ....

ADDRESS I ....

ADDRESS 2 ....

POST CODE .... GPS ....

E MAIL .... PHONE ....

WEBSITE WWW...

MY RATING ☆☆☆☆☆☆☆☆☆☆ RECOMMEND YES/NO

WHAT 3 WORDS LOCATION ....

NUMBER OF NIGHTS HERE ....

PEOPLE WE MET - NAMES, E MAIL, PHONE NUMBER

....
....
....
....

DAILY COSTS

			TODAY'S HIGHLIGHTS
SITE FEES	£	....	....
FUEL	£	....	....
LPG GAS	£	....	....
TOLLS	£	....	....
GROCERIES	£	....	....
EATING OUT	£	....	....
ENTERTAINMENT	£	....	....
OTHER COSTS	£	....	....

NOTES

....
....
....
....
....

CAMPING TRAVEL JOURNAL

DATE   ..../..../.........   MILEAGE START ....

START TIME   ....   MILEAGE END   ....

ARRIVAL TIME ....   MILEAGE TOTAL ....

CAMPSITE NAME ....

ADDRESS I ....

ADDRESS 2 ....

POST CODE ....   GPS ....

E MAIL ....   PHONE ....

WEBSITE WWW...

MY RATING ☆☆☆☆☆☆☆☆☆☆   RECOMMEND YES/NO

WHAT 3 WORDS LOCATION ....

NUMBER OF NIGHTS HERE ....

PEOPLE WE MET - NAMES, E MAIL, PHONE NUMBER

....

....

....

....

DAILY COSTS		TODAY'S HIGHLIGHTS
SITE FEES	£	....
FUEL	£	....
LPG GAS	£	....
TOLLS	£	....
GROCERIES	£	....
EATING OUT	£	....
ENTERTAINMENT	£	....
OTHER COSTS	£	....

NOTES

....

....

....

....

....

CAMPING TRAVEL JOURNAL

DATE ..../..../......... MILEAGE START ....

START TIME .... MILEAGE END ....

ARRIVAL TIME .... MILEAGE TOTAL ....

CAMPSITE NAME ....

ADDRESS 1 ....

ADDRESS 2 ....

POST CODE .... GPS ....

E MAIL .... PHONE ....

WEBSITE WWW...

MY RATING ☆☆☆☆☆☆☆☆☆☆ RECOMMEND YES/NO

WHAT 3 WORDS LOCATION ....

NUMBER OF NIGHTS HERE ....

PEOPLE WE MET - NAMES, E MAIL, PHONE NUMBER

....
....
....
....

DAILY COSTS		TODAY'S HIGHLIGHTS
SITE FEES	£	....
FUEL	£	....
LPG GAS	£	....
TOLLS	£	....
GROCERIES	£	....
EATING OUT	£	....
ENTERTAINMENT	£	....
OTHER COSTS	£	....

NOTES

....
....
....
....
....

CAMPING TRAVEL JOURNAL

DATE   ..../..../......... MILEAGE START ....
START TIME .... MILEAGE END ....
ARRIVAL TIME .... MILEAGE TOTAL ....

CAMPSITE NAME ....
ADDRESS 1 ....
ADDRESS 2 ....
POST CODE .... GPS ....
E MAIL .... PHONE ....
WEBSITE WWW..
MY RATING ☆☆☆☆☆☆☆☆☆☆   RECOMMEND YES/NO
WHAT 3 WORDS LOCATION ....
NUMBER OF NIGHTS HERE ....

PEOPLE WE MET - NAMES, E MAIL, PHONE NUMBER
....
....
....
....

DAILY COSTS		TODAY'S HIGHLIGHTS
SITE FEES	£	....
FUEL	£	....
LPG GAS	£	....
TOLLS	£	....
GROCERIES	£	....
EATING OUT	£	....
ENTERTAINMENT	£	....
OTHER COSTS	£	....

NOTES
....
....
....
....
....

CAMPING TRAVEL JOURNAL

DATE ..../..../......... MILEAGE START ....

START TIME .... MILEAGE END ....

ARRIVAL TIME .... MILEAGE TOTAL ....

CAMPSITE NAME ....

ADDRESS I ....

ADDRESS 2 ....

POST CODE .... GPS ....

E MAIL .... PHONE ....

WEBSITE WWW...

MY RATING ☆☆☆☆☆☆☆☆☆☆ RECOMMEND YES/NO

WHAT 3 WORDS LOCATION ....

NUMBER OF NIGHTS HERE ....

PEOPLE WE MET - NAMES, E MAIL, PHONE NUMBER

....

....

....

....

DAILY COSTS		TODAY'S HIGHLIGHTS
SITE FEES	£	....
FUEL	£	....
LPG GAS	£	....
TOLLS	£	....
GROCERIES	£	....
EATING OUT	£	....
ENTERTAINMENT	£	....
OTHER COSTS	£	....

NOTES

....

....

....

....

....

CAMPING TRAVEL JOURNAL

DATE ..../..../......... MILEAGE START ....

START TIME .... MILEAGE END ....

ARRIVAL TIME .... MILEAGE TOTAL ....

CAMPSITE NAME ....

ADDRESS 1 ....

ADDRESS 2 ....

POST CODE .... GPS ....

E MAIL .... PHONE ....

WEBSITE WWW...

MY RATING ☆☆☆☆☆☆☆☆☆☆ RECOMMEND YES/NO

WHAT 3 WORDS LOCATION ....

NUMBER OF NIGHTS HERE ....

PEOPLE WE MET - NAMES, E MAIL, PHONE NUMBER

....

....

....

....

DAILY COSTS		TODAY'S HIGHLIGHTS
SITE FEES	£	....
FUEL	£	....
LPG GAS	£	....
TOLLS	£	....
GROCERIES	£	....
EATING OUT	£	....
ENTERTAINMENT	£	....
OTHER COSTS	£	....

NOTES

....

....

....

....

....

CAMPING TRAVEL JOURNAL

DATE ..../..../........ MILEAGE START ....

START TIME .... MILEAGE END ....

ARRIVAL TIME .... MILEAGE TOTAL ....

CAMPSITE NAME ....

ADDRESS 1 ....

ADDRESS 2 ....

POST CODE .... GPS ....

E MAIL .... PHONE ....

WEBSITE WWW...

MY RATING ☆☆☆☆☆☆☆☆☆☆ RECOMMEND YES/NO

WHAT 3 WORDS LOCATION ....

NUMBER OF NIGHTS HERE ....

PEOPLE WE MET - NAMES, E MAIL, PHONE NUMBER

....

....

....

....

DAILY COSTS		TODAY'S HIGHLIGHTS
SITE FEES	£	....
FUEL	£	....
LPG GAS	£	....
TOLLS	£	....
GROCERIES	£	....
EATING OUT	£	....
ENTERTAINMENT	£	....
OTHER COSTS	£	....

NOTES

....

....

....

....

....

CAMPING TRAVEL JOURNAL

DATE ..../..../........ MILEAGE START ....

START TIME .... MILEAGE END ....

ARRIVAL TIME .... MILEAGE TOTAL ....

CAMPSITE NAME ....

ADDRESS 1 ....

ADDRESS 2 ....

POST CODE .... GPS ....

E MAIL .... PHONE ....

WEBSITE WWW...

MY RATING ☆☆☆☆☆☆☆☆☆☆ RECOMMEND YES/NO

WHAT 3 WORDS LOCATION ....

NUMBER OF NIGHTS HERE ....

PEOPLE WE MET - NAMES, E MAIL, PHONE NUMBER

....

....

....

....

DAILY COSTS

SITE FEES	£	....
FUEL	£	....
LPG GAS	£	....
TOLLS	£	....
GROCERIES	£	....
EATING OUT	£	....
ENTERTAINMENT	£	....
OTHER COSTS	£	....

TODAY'S HIGHLIGHTS

....

....

....

....

....

....

....

NOTES

....

....

....

....

....

CAMPING TRAVEL JOURNAL

DATE ..../..../......... MILEAGE START ....

START TIME .... MILEAGE END ....

ARRIVAL TIME .... MILEAGE TOTAL ....

CAMPSITE NAME ....

ADDRESS 1 ....

ADDRESS 2 ....

POST CODE .... GPS ....

E MAIL .... PHONE ....

WEBSITE WWW..

MY RATING ☆☆☆☆☆☆☆☆☆☆ RECOMMEND YES/NO

WHAT 3 WORDS LOCATION ....

NUMBER OF NIGHTS HERE ....

PEOPLE WE MET - NAMES, E MAIL, PHONE NUMBER

....

....

....

....

DAILY COSTS		TODAY'S HIGHLIGHTS
SITE FEES	£	....
FUEL	£	....
LPG GAS	£	....
TOLLS	£	....
GROCERIES	£	....
EATING OUT	£	....
ENTERTAINMENT	£	....
OTHER COSTS	£	....

NOTES

....

....

....

....

....

CAMPING TRAVEL JOURNAL

DATE ..../..../......... MILEAGE START ....

START TIME .... MILEAGE END ....

ARRIVAL TIME .... MILEAGE TOTAL ....

CAMPSITE NAME ....

ADDRESS 1 ....

ADDRESS 2 ....

POST CODE .... GPS ....

E MAIL .... PHONE ....

WEBSITE WWW..

MY RATING ☆☆☆☆☆☆☆☆☆☆ RECOMMEND YES/NO

WHAT 3 WORDS LOCATION ....

NUMBER OF NIGHTS HERE ....

PEOPLE WE MET - NAMES, E MAIL, PHONE NUMBER

....
....
....
....

DAILY COSTS		TODAY'S HIGHLIGHTS
SITE FEES	£	....
FUEL	£	....
LPG GAS	£	....
TOLLS	£	....
GROCERIES	£	....
EATING OUT	£	....
ENTERTAINMENT	£	....
OTHER COSTS	£	....

NOTES

....
....
....
....
....

CAMPING TRAVEL JOURNAL

DATE ..../..../.........   MILEAGE START ....

START TIME ....   MILEAGE END ....

ARRIVAL TIME ....   MILEAGE TOTAL ....

CAMPSITE NAME ....

ADDRESS I ....

ADDRESS 2 ....

POST CODE ....   GPS ....

E MAIL ....   PHONE ....

WEBSITE WWW...

MY RATING ☆☆☆☆☆☆☆☆☆☆   RECOMMEND YES/NO

WHAT 3 WORDS LOCATION ....

NUMBER OF NIGHTS HERE ....

PEOPLE WE MET - NAMES, E MAIL, PHONE NUMBER
....
....
....
....

DAILY COSTS		TODAY'S HIGHLIGHTS
SITE FEES	£	....
FUEL	£	....
LPG GAS	£	....
TOLLS	£	....
GROCERIES	£	....
EATING OUT	£	....
ENTERTAINMENT	£	....
OTHER COSTS	£	....

NOTES
....
....
....
....
....

CAMPING TRAVEL JOURNAL

DATE ..../..../......... MILEAGE START ....

START TIME .... MILEAGE END ....

ARRIVAL TIME .... MILEAGE TOTAL ....

CAMPSITE NAME ....

ADDRESS 1 ....

ADDRESS 2 ....

POST CODE .... GPS ....

E MAIL .... PHONE ....

WEBSITE WWW...

MY RATING ☆☆☆☆☆☆☆☆☆☆ RECOMMEND YES/NO

WHAT 3 WORDS LOCATION ....

NUMBER OF NIGHTS HERE ....

PEOPLE WE MET - NAMES, E MAIL, PHONE NUMBER

....

....

....

....

DAILY COSTS		TODAY'S HIGHLIGHTS
SITE FEES	£	....
FUEL	£	....
LPG GAS	£	....
TOLLS	£	....
GROCERIES	£	....
EATING OUT	£	....
ENTERTAINMENT	£	....
OTHER COSTS	£	....

NOTES

....

....

....

....

....

CAMPING TRAVEL JOURNAL

DATE ..../..../......... MILEAGE START ....

START TIME .... MILEAGE END ....

ARRIVAL TIME .... MILEAGE TOTAL ....

CAMPSITE NAME ....

ADDRESS I ....

ADDRESS 2 ....

POST CODE .... GPS ....

E MAIL .... PHONE ....

WEBSITE WWW...

MY RATING ☆☆☆☆☆☆☆☆☆☆ RECOMMEND YES/NO

WHAT 3 WORDS LOCATION ....

NUMBER OF NIGHTS HERE ....

PEOPLE WE MET - NAMES, E MAIL, PHONE NUMBER

....

....

....

....

DAILY COSTS

		TODAY'S HIGHLIGHTS
SITE FEES	£	....
FUEL	£	....
LPG GAS	£	....
TOLLS	£	....
GROCERIES	£	....
EATING OUT	£	....
ENTERTAINMENT	£	....
OTHER COSTS	£	....

NOTES

....

....

....

....

....

CAMPING TRAVEL JOURNAL

DATE ..../..../......... MILEAGE START ....

START TIME .... MILEAGE END ....

ARRIVAL TIME .... MILEAGE TOTAL ....

CAMPSITE NAME ....

ADDRESS 1 ....

ADDRESS 2 ....

POST CODE .... GPS ....

E MAIL .... PHONE ....

WEBSITE WWW...

MY RATING ☆☆☆☆☆☆☆☆☆☆   RECOMMEND YES/NO

WHAT 3 WORDS LOCATION ....

NUMBER OF NIGHTS HERE ....

PEOPLE WE MET - NAMES, E MAIL, PHONE NUMBER

....

....

....

....

DAILY COSTS			TODAY'S HIGHLIGHTS
SITE FEES	£	....	....
FUEL	£	....	....
LPG GAS	£	....	....
TOLLS	£	....	....
GROCERIES	£	....	....
EATING OUT	£	....	....
ENTERTAINMENT	£	....	....
OTHER COSTS	£	....	....

NOTES

....

....

....

....

....

CAMPING TRAVEL JOURNAL

DATE ..../..../......... MILEAGE START ....

START TIME .... MILEAGE END ....

ARRIVAL TIME .... MILEAGE TOTAL ....

CAMPSITE NAME ....

ADDRESS 1 ....

ADDRESS 2 ....

POST CODE .... GPS ....

E MAIL .... PHONE ....

WEBSITE WWW...

MY RATING ☆☆☆☆☆☆☆☆☆☆ RECOMMEND YES/NO

WHAT 3 WORDS LOCATION ....

NUMBER OF NIGHTS HERE ....

PEOPLE WE MET - NAMES, E MAIL, PHONE NUMBER

....
....
....
....

DAILY COSTS		TODAY'S HIGHLIGHTS
SITE FEES	£	....
FUEL	£	....
LPG GAS	£	....
TOLLS	£	....
GROCERIES	£	....
EATING OUT	£	....
ENTERTAINMENT	£	....
OTHER COSTS	£	....

NOTES

....
....
....
....
....

CAMPING TRAVEL JOURNAL

DATE ..../..../......... MILEAGE START ....

START TIME .... MILEAGE END ....

ARRIVAL TIME .... MILEAGE TOTAL ....

CAMPSITE NAME ....

ADDRESS I ....

ADDRESS 2 ....

POST CODE .... GPS ....

E MAIL .... PHONE ....

WEBSITE WWW..

MY RATING ☆☆☆☆☆☆☆☆☆☆ RECOMMEND YES/NO

WHAT 3 WORDS LOCATION ....

NUMBER OF NIGHTS HERE ....

PEOPLE WE MET - NAMES, E MAIL, PHONE NUMBER

....

....

....

....

DAILY COSTS		TODAY'S HIGHLIGHTS
SITE FEES	£	....
FUEL	£	....
LPG GAS	£	....
TOLLS	£	....
GROCERIES	£	....
EATING OUT	£	....
ENTERTAINMENT	£	....
OTHER COSTS	£	....

NOTES

....

....

....

....

....

CAMPING TRAVEL JOURNAL

DATE ...../...../......... MILEAGE START ....

START TIME .... MILEAGE END ....

ARRIVAL TIME .... MILEAGE TOTAL ....

CAMPSITE NAME ....

ADDRESS I ....

ADDRESS 2 ....

POST CODE .... GPS ....

E MAIL .... PHONE ....

WEBSITE WWW...

MY RATING ☆ ☆ ☆ ☆ ☆ ☆ ☆ ☆ ☆ ☆   RECOMMEND YES/NO

WHAT 3 WORDS LOCATION ....

NUMBER OF NIGHTS HERE ....

PEOPLE WE MET - NAMES, E MAIL, PHONE NUMBER

....

....

....

....

DAILY COSTS		TODAY'S HIGHLIGHTS
SITE FEES	£	....
FUEL	£	....
LPG GAS	£	....
TOLLS	£	....
GROCERIES	£	....
EATING OUT	£	....
ENTERTAINMENT	£	....
OTHER COSTS	£	....

NOTES

....

....

....

....

....

CAMPING TRAVEL JOURNAL

DATE ..../..../......... MILEAGE START ....

START TIME .... MILEAGE END ....

ARRIVAL TIME .... MILEAGE TOTAL ....

CAMPSITE NAME ....

ADDRESS 1 ....

ADDRESS 2 ....

POST CODE .... GPS ....

E MAIL .... PHONE ....

WEBSITE WWW...

MY RATING ☆☆☆☆☆☆☆☆☆☆ RECOMMEND YES/NO

WHAT 3 WORDS LOCATION ....

NUMBER OF NIGHTS HERE ....

PEOPLE WE MET - NAMES, E MAIL, PHONE NUMBER

....

....

....

....

DAILY COSTS		TODAY'S HIGHLIGHTS
SITE FEES	£	....
FUEL	£	....
LPG GAS	£	....
TOLLS	£	....
GROCERIES	£	....
EATING OUT	£	....
ENTERTAINMENT	£	....
OTHER COSTS	£	....

NOTES

....

....

....

....

....

CAMPING TRAVEL JOURNAL

DATE ..../..../......... MILEAGE START ....

START TIME .... MILEAGE END ....

ARRIVAL TIME .... MILEAGE TOTAL ....

CAMPSITE NAME ....

ADDRESS 1 ....

ADDRESS 2 ....

POST CODE .... GPS ....

E MAIL .... PHONE ....

WEBSITE WWW...

MY RATING ☆ ☆ ☆ ☆ ☆ ☆ ☆ ☆ ☆ ☆   RECOMMEND YES/NO

WHAT 3 WORDS LOCATION ....

NUMBER OF NIGHTS HERE ....

PEOPLE WE MET - NAMES, E MAIL, PHONE NUMBER

....

....

....

....

DAILY COSTS		TODAY'S HIGHLIGHTS
SITE FEES	£	....
FUEL	£	....
LPG GAS	£	....
TOLLS	£	....
GROCERIES	£	....
EATING OUT	£	....
ENTERTAINMENT	£	....
OTHER COSTS	£	....

NOTES

....

....

....

....

....

CAMPING TRAVEL JOURNAL

DATE   ..../..../.........   MILEAGE START ....

START TIME   ....   MILEAGE END   ....

ARRIVAL TIME ....   MILEAGE TOTAL ....

CAMPSITE NAME ....

ADDRESS 1 ....

ADDRESS 2 ....

POST CODE ....   GPS ....

E MAIL ....   PHONE ....

WEBSITE WWW...

MY RATING ☆☆☆☆☆☆☆☆☆☆   RECOMMEND YES/NO

WHAT 3 WORDS LOCATION ....

NUMBER OF NIGHTS HERE ....

PEOPLE WE MET - NAMES, E MAIL, PHONE NUMBER

....
....
....
....

DAILY COSTS		TODAY'S HIGHLIGHTS
SITE FEES	£	....
FUEL	£	....
LPG GAS	£	....
TOLLS	£	....
GROCERIES	£	....
EATING OUT	£	....
ENTERTAINMENT	£	....
OTHER COSTS	£	....

NOTES

....
....
....
....
....

CAMPING TRAVEL JOURNAL

DATE ..../..../......... MILEAGE START ....

START TIME .... MILEAGE END ....

ARRIVAL TIME .... MILEAGE TOTAL ....

CAMPSITE NAME ....

ADDRESS 1 ....

ADDRESS 2 ....

POST CODE .... GPS ....

E MAIL .... PHONE ....

WEBSITE WWW...

MY RATING ☆☆☆☆☆☆☆☆☆☆ RECOMMEND YES/NO

WHAT 3 WORDS LOCATION ....

NUMBER OF NIGHTS HERE ....

PEOPLE WE MET - NAMES, E MAIL, PHONE NUMBER
....
....
....
....

DAILY COSTS

SITE FEES	£	....
FUEL	£	....
LPG GAS	£	....
TOLLS	£	....
GROCERIES	£	....
EATING OUT	£	....
ENTERTAINMENT	£	....
OTHER COSTS	£	....

TODAY'S HIGHLIGHTS
....
....
....
....
....
....
....

NOTES
....
....
....
....
....
....

CAMPING TRAVEL JOURNAL

DATE   ..../..../.........   MILEAGE START ....
START TIME   ....   MILEAGE END   ....
ARRIVAL TIME ....   MILEAGE TOTAL ....

CAMPSITE NAME ....
ADDRESS 1 ....
ADDRESS 2 ....
POST CODE ....   GPS ....
E MAIL ....   PHONE ....
WEBSITE WWW...
MY RATING ☆☆☆☆☆☆☆☆☆☆   RECOMMEND YES/NO
WHAT 3 WORDS LOCATION ....
NUMBER OF NIGHTS HERE ....

PEOPLE WE MET - NAMES, E MAIL, PHONE NUMBER
....
....
....
....

DAILY COSTS		TODAY'S HIGHLIGHTS
SITE FEES	£	....
FUEL	£	....
LPG GAS	£	....
TOLLS	£	....
GROCERIES	£	....
EATING OUT	£	....
ENTERTAINMENT	£	....
OTHER COSTS	£	....

NOTES
....
....
....
....
....

CAMPING TRAVEL JOURNAL

DATE ...../...../......... MILEAGE START ....

START TIME .... MILEAGE END ....

ARRIVAL TIME .... MILEAGE TOTAL ....

CAMPSITE NAME ....

ADDRESS 1 ....

ADDRESS 2 ....

POST CODE .... GPS ....

E MAIL .... PHONE ....

WEBSITE WWW..

MY RATING ☆☆☆☆☆☆☆☆☆☆ RECOMMEND YES/NO

WHAT 3 WORDS LOCATION ....

NUMBER OF NIGHTS HERE ....

PEOPLE WE MET - NAMES, E MAIL, PHONE NUMBER

....

....

....

....

DAILY COSTS		TODAY'S HIGHLIGHTS
SITE FEES	£	....
FUEL	£	....
LPG GAS	£	....
TOLLS	£	....
GROCERIES	£	....
EATING OUT	£	....
ENTERTAINMENT	£	....
OTHER COSTS	£	....

NOTES

....

....

....

....

....

CAMPING TRAVEL JOURNAL

DATE ..../..../......... MILEAGE START ....

START TIME .... MILEAGE END ....

ARRIVAL TIME .... MILEAGE TOTAL ....

CAMPSITE NAME ....

ADDRESS 1 ....

ADDRESS 2 ....

POST CODE .... GPS ....

E MAIL .... PHONE ....

WEBSITE WWW...

MY RATING ☆☆☆☆☆☆☆☆☆☆ RECOMMEND YES/NO

WHAT 3 WORDS LOCATION ....

NUMBER OF NIGHTS HERE ....

PEOPLE WE MET - NAMES, E MAIL, PHONE NUMBER

....

....

....

....

DAILY COSTS		TODAY'S HIGHLIGHTS
SITE FEES	£	....
FUEL	£	....
LPG GAS	£	....
TOLLS	£	....
GROCERIES	£	....
EATING OUT	£	....
ENTERTAINMENT	£	....
OTHER COSTS	£	....

NOTES

....

....

....

....

....

CAMPING TRAVEL JOURNAL

DATE ..../..../......... MILEAGE START ....

START TIME .... MILEAGE END ....

ARRIVAL TIME .... MILEAGE TOTAL ....

CAMPSITE NAME ....

ADDRESS 1 ....

ADDRESS 2 ....

POST CODE .... GPS ....

E MAIL .... PHONE ....

WEBSITE WWW...

MY RATING ☆☆☆☆☆☆☆☆☆☆ RECOMMEND YES/NO

WHAT 3 WORDS LOCATION ....

NUMBER OF NIGHTS HERE ....

PEOPLE WE MET - NAMES, E MAIL, PHONE NUMBER

....

....

....

....

DAILY COSTS		TODAY'S HIGHLIGHTS
SITE FEES	£	....
FUEL	£	....
LPG GAS	£	....
TOLLS	£	....
GROCERIES	£	....
EATING OUT	£	....
ENTERTAINMENT	£	....
OTHER COSTS	£	....

NOTES

....

....

....

....

....

CAMPING TRAVEL JOURNAL

DATE ..../..../......... MILEAGE START ....

START TIME .... MILEAGE END ....

ARRIVAL TIME .... MILEAGE TOTAL ....

CAMPSITE NAME ....

ADDRESS 1 ....

ADDRESS 2 ....

POST CODE .... GPS ....

E MAIL .... PHONE ....

WEBSITE WWW..

MY RATING ☆☆☆☆☆☆☆☆☆☆ RECOMMEND YES/NO

WHAT 3 WORDS LOCATION ....

NUMBER OF NIGHTS HERE ....

PEOPLE WE MET - NAMES, E MAIL, PHONE NUMBER

....
....
....
....

DAILY COSTS

SITE FEES £ ....

FUEL £ ....

LPG GAS £ ....

TOLLS £ ....

GROCERIES £ ....

EATING OUT £ ....

ENTERTAINMENT £ ....

OTHER COSTS £ ....

TODAY'S HIGHLIGHTS

....
....
....
....
....
....
....

NOTES

....
....
....
....
....

CAMPING TRAVEL JOURNAL

DATE ..../..../......... MILEAGE START ....

START TIME .... MILEAGE END ....

ARRIVAL TIME .... MILEAGE TOTAL ....

CAMPSITE NAME ....

ADDRESS 1 ....

ADDRESS 2 ....

POST CODE .... GPS ....

E MAIL .... PHONE ....

WEBSITE WWW...

MY RATING ☆☆☆☆☆☆☆☆☆☆   RECOMMEND YES/NO

WHAT 3 WORDS LOCATION ....

NUMBER OF NIGHTS HERE ....

PEOPLE WE MET - NAMES, E MAIL, PHONE NUMBER

....

....

....

....

DAILY COSTS		TODAY'S HIGHLIGHTS
SITE FEES	£	....
FUEL	£	....
LPG GAS	£	....
TOLLS	£	....
GROCERIES	£	....
EATING OUT	£	....
ENTERTAINMENT	£	....
OTHER COSTS	£	....

NOTES

....

....

....

....

....

CAMPING TRAVEL JOURNAL

DATE ..../..../......... MILEAGE START ....

START TIME .... MILEAGE END ....

ARRIVAL TIME .... MILEAGE TOTAL ....

CAMPSITE NAME ....

ADDRESS 1 ....

ADDRESS 2 ....

POST CODE .... GPS ....

E MAIL .... PHONE ....

WEBSITE WWW..

MY RATING ☆☆☆☆☆☆☆☆☆☆ RECOMMEND YES/NO

WHAT 3 WORDS LOCATION ....

NUMBER OF NIGHTS HERE ......

PEOPLE WE MET - NAMES, E MAIL, PHONE NUMBER

....

....

....

....

DAILY COSTS		TODAY'S HIGHLIGHTS
SITE FEES	£	....
FUEL	£	....
LPG GAS	£	....
TOLLS	£	....
GROCERIES	£	....
EATING OUT	£	....
ENTERTAINMENT	£	....
OTHER COSTS	£	....

NOTES

....

....

....

....

....

CAMPING TRAVEL JOURNAL

DATE ..../..../......... MILEAGE START ....

START TIME .... MILEAGE END ....

ARRIVAL TIME .... MILEAGE TOTAL ....

CAMPSITE NAME ....

ADDRESS 1 ....

ADDRESS 2 ....

POST CODE .... GPS ....

E MAIL .... PHONE ....

WEBSITE WWW..

MY RATING ☆☆☆☆☆☆☆☆☆☆ RECOMMEND YES/NO

WHAT 3 WORDS LOCATION ....

NUMBER OF NIGHTS HERE ....

PEOPLE WE MET - NAMES, E MAIL, PHONE NUMBER

....

....

....

....

DAILY COSTS		TODAY'S HIGHLIGHTS
SITE FEES	£	....
FUEL	£	....
LPG GAS	£	....
TOLLS	£	....
GROCERIES	£	....
EATING OUT	£	....
ENTERTAINMENT	£	....
OTHER COSTS	£	....

NOTES

....

....

....

....

....

CAMPING TRAVEL JOURNAL

DATE   ..../..../........   MILEAGE START ....

START TIME   ....   MILEAGE END   ....

ARRIVAL TIME ....   MILEAGE TOTAL ....

CAMPSITE NAME ....

ADDRESS 1 ....

ADDRESS 2 ....

POST CODE ....   GPS ....

E MAIL ....   PHONE ....

WEBSITE WWW..

MY RATING ☆☆☆☆☆☆☆☆☆☆   RECOMMEND YES/NO

WHAT 3 WORDS LOCATION ....

NUMBER OF NIGHTS HERE ....

PEOPLE WE MET - NAMES, E MAIL, PHONE NUMBER

....

....

....

....

DAILY COSTS		TODAY'S HIGHLIGHTS
SITE FEES	£	....
FUEL	£	....
LPG GAS	£	....
TOLLS	£	....
GROCERIES	£	....
EATING OUT	£	....
ENTERTAINMENT £		....
OTHER COSTS	£	....

NOTES

....

....

....

....

....

CAMPING TRAVEL JOURNAL

DATE   ..../..../......... MILEAGE START ....

START TIME ....   MILEAGE END   ....

ARRIVAL TIME ....   MILEAGE TOTAL ....

CAMPSITE NAME ....

ADDRESS 1 ....

ADDRESS 2 ....

POST CODE ....   GPS ....

E MAIL ....   PHONE ....

WEBSITE WWW...

MY RATING ☆☆☆☆☆☆☆☆☆☆   RECOMMEND YES/NO

WHAT 3 WORDS LOCATION ....

NUMBER OF NIGHTS HERE ....

PEOPLE WE MET - NAMES, E MAIL, PHONE NUMBER

....

....

....

....

DAILY COSTS		TODAY'S HIGHLIGHTS
SITE FEES	£	....
FUEL	£	....
LPG GAS	£	....
TOLLS	£	....
GROCERIES	£	....
EATING OUT	£	....
ENTERTAINMENT	£	....
OTHER COSTS	£	....

NOTES

....

....

....

....

....

CAMPING TRAVEL JOURNAL

DATE ..../..../........ MILEAGE START ....

START TIME .... MILEAGE END ....

ARRIVAL TIME .... MILEAGE TOTAL ....

___

CAMPSITE NAME ....

ADDRESS 1 ....

ADDRESS 2 ....

POST CODE .... GPS ....

E MAIL .... PHONE ....

WEBSITE WWW...

MY RATING ☆☆☆☆☆☆☆☆☆☆ RECOMMEND YES/NO

WHAT 3 WORDS LOCATION ....

NUMBER OF NIGHTS HERE ....

___

PEOPLE WE MET - NAMES, E MAIL, PHONE NUMBER

....
....
....
....

___

DAILY COSTS		TODAY'S HIGHLIGHTS
SITE FEES	£	....
FUEL	£	....
LPG GAS	£	....
TOLLS	£	....
GROCERIES	£	....
EATING OUT	£	....
ENTERTAINMENT	£	....
OTHER COSTS	£	....

NOTES

....
....
....
....
....

CAMPING TRAVEL JOURNAL

DATE   ..../..../.........   MILEAGE START ....

START TIME   ....   MILEAGE END   ....

ARRIVAL TIME ....   MILEAGE TOTAL ....

CAMPSITE NAME ....

ADDRESS 1 ....

ADDRESS 2 ....

POST CODE ....   GPS ....

E MAIL ....   PHONE ....

WEBSITE WWW...

MY RATING ☆ ☆ ☆ ☆ ☆ ☆ ☆ ☆ ☆ ☆   RECOMMEND YES/NO

WHAT 3 WORDS LOCATION ....

NUMBER OF NIGHTS HERE ....

PEOPLE WE MET - NAMES, E MAIL, PHONE NUMBER

....

....

....

....

DAILY COSTS		TODAY'S HIGHLIGHTS
SITE FEES	£	....
FUEL	£	....
LPG GAS	£	....
TOLLS	£	....
GROCERIES	£	....
EATING OUT	£	....
ENTERTAINMENT	£	....
OTHER COSTS	£	....

NOTES

....

....

....

....

....

CAMPING TRAVEL JOURNAL

DATE   ..../..../.........   MILEAGE START ....

START TIME   ....   MILEAGE END   ....

ARRIVAL TIME ....   MILEAGE TOTAL ....

CAMPSITE NAME ....

ADDRESS 1 ....

ADDRESS 2 ....

POST CODE ....   GPS ....

E MAIL ....   PHONE ....

WEBSITE WWW..

MY RATING ☆☆☆☆☆☆☆☆☆☆   RECOMMEND YES/NO

WHAT 3 WORDS LOCATION ....

NUMBER OF NIGHTS HERE ......

PEOPLE WE MET - NAMES, E MAIL, PHONE NUMBER

....
....
....
....

DAILY COSTS		TODAY'S HIGHLIGHTS
SITE FEES	£	....
FUEL	£	....
LPG GAS	£	....
TOLLS	£	....
GROCERIES	£	....
EATING OUT	£	....
ENTERTAINMENT	£	....
OTHER COSTS	£	....

NOTES

....
....
....
....
....

CAMPING TRAVEL JOURNAL

DATE ..../..../......... MILEAGE START ....

START TIME .... MILEAGE END ....

ARRIVAL TIME .... MILEAGE TOTAL ....

CAMPSITE NAME ....

ADDRESS 1 ....

ADDRESS 2 ....

POST CODE .... GPS ....

E MAIL .... PHONE ....

WEBSITE WWW...

MY RATING ☆☆☆☆☆☆☆☆☆☆ RECOMMEND YES/NO

WHAT 3 WORDS LOCATION ....

NUMBER OF NIGHTS HERE ....

PEOPLE WE MET - NAMES, E MAIL, PHONE NUMBER

....
....
....
....

DAILY COSTS		TODAY'S HIGHLIGHTS
SITE FEES	£	....
FUEL	£	....
LPG GAS	£	....
TOLLS	£	....
GROCERIES	£	....
EATING OUT	£	....
ENTERTAINMENT	£	....
OTHER COSTS	£	....

NOTES

....
....
....
....
....

CAMPING TRAVEL JOURNAL

DATE ..../..../.........   MILEAGE START ....

START TIME ....   MILEAGE END ....

ARRIVAL TIME ....   MILEAGE TOTAL ....

CAMPSITE NAME ....

ADDRESS 1 ....

ADDRESS 2 ....

POST CODE ....   GPS ....

E MAIL ....   PHONE ....

WEBSITE WWW...

MY RATING ☆☆☆☆☆☆☆☆☆☆   RECOMMEND YES/NO

WHAT 3 WORDS LOCATION ....

NUMBER OF NIGHTS HERE ....

PEOPLE WE MET - NAMES, E MAIL, PHONE NUMBER

....

....

....

....

DAILY COSTS		TODAY'S HIGHLIGHTS
SITE FEES	£	....
FUEL	£	....
LPG GAS	£	....
TOLLS	£	....
GROCERIES	£	....
EATING OUT	£	....
ENTERTAINMENT	£	....
OTHER COSTS	£	....

NOTES

....

....

....

....

....

CAMPING TRAVEL JOURNAL

DATE ..../..../......... MILEAGE START ....
START TIME .... MILEAGE END ....
ARRIVAL TIME .... MILEAGE TOTAL ....

CAMPSITE NAME ....
ADDRESS I ....
ADDRESS 2 ....
POST CODE .... GPS ....
E MAIL .... PHONE ....
WEBSITE WWW..
MY RATING ☆☆☆☆☆☆☆☆☆☆ RECOMMEND YES/NO
WHAT 3 WORDS LOCATION ....
NUMBER OF NIGHTS HERE ....

PEOPLE WE MET - NAMES, E MAIL, PHONE NUMBER
....
....
....
....

DAILY COSTS   TODAY'S HIGHLIGHTS

SITE FEES   £ ....
FUEL   £ ....
LPG GAS   £ ....
TOLLS   £ ....
GROCERIES   £ ....
EATING OUT   £ ....
ENTERTAINMENT   £ ....
OTHER COSTS   £ ....

NOTES

....
....
....
....
....

CAMPING TRAVEL JOURNAL

DATE ..../..../........ MILEAGE START ....

START TIME .... MILEAGE END ....

ARRIVAL TIME .... MILEAGE TOTAL ....

CAMPSITE NAME ....

ADDRESS 1 ....

ADDRESS 2 ....

POST CODE .... GPS ....

E MAIL .... PHONE ....

WEBSITE WWW..

MY RATING ☆☆☆☆☆☆☆☆☆☆ RECOMMEND YES/NO

WHAT 3 WORDS LOCATION ....

NUMBER OF NIGHTS HERE ....

PEOPLE WE MET - NAMES, E MAIL, PHONE NUMBER

....
....
....
....

DAILY COSTS

		TODAY'S HIGHLIGHTS
SITE FEES	£	....
FUEL	£	....
LPG GAS	£	....
TOLLS	£	....
GROCERIES	£	....
EATING OUT	£	....
ENTERTAINMENT	£	....
OTHER COSTS	£	....

NOTES

....
....
....
....
....

CAMPING TRAVEL JOURNAL

DATE ...../...../.......... MILEAGE START ....

START TIME .... MILEAGE END ....

ARRIVAL TIME .... MILEAGE TOTAL ....

CAMPSITE NAME ....

ADDRESS 1 ....

ADDRESS 2 ....

POST CODE .... GPS ....

E MAIL .... PHONE ....

WEBSITE WWW..

MY RATING ☆ ☆ ☆ ☆ ☆ ☆ ☆ ☆ ☆ ☆   RECOMMEND YES/NO

WHAT 3 WORDS LOCATION ....

NUMBER OF NIGHTS HERE ....

PEOPLE WE MET - NAMES, E MAIL, PHONE NUMBER

....
....
....
....

DAILY COSTS		TODAY'S HIGHLIGHTS
SITE FEES	£	....
FUEL	£	....
LPG GAS	£	....
TOLLS	£	....
GROCERIES	£	....
EATING OUT	£	....
ENTERTAINMENT	£	....
OTHER COSTS	£	....

NOTES

....
....
....
....
....

CAMPING TRAVEL JOURNAL

DATE ..../..../......... MILEAGE START ....

START TIME .... MILEAGE END ....

ARRIVAL TIME .... MILEAGE TOTAL ....

CAMPSITE NAME ....

ADDRESS 1 ....

ADDRESS 2 ....

POST CODE .... GPS ....

E MAIL .... PHONE ....

WEBSITE WWW...

MY RATING ☆☆☆☆☆☆☆☆☆☆ RECOMMEND YES/NO

WHAT 3 WORDS LOCATION ....

NUMBER OF NIGHTS HERE ....

PEOPLE WE MET - NAMES, E MAIL, PHONE NUMBER

....
....
....
....

DAILY COSTS

SITE FEES   £ ....

FUEL   £ ....

LPG GAS   £ ....

TOLLS   £ ....

GROCERIES   £ ....

EATING OUT   £ ....

ENTERTAINMENT £ ....

OTHER COSTS   £ ....

TODAY'S HIGHLIGHTS

....
....
....
....
....
....
....

NOTES

....
....
....
....
....

CAMPING TRAVEL JOURNAL

DATE ..../..../......... MILEAGE START ....

START TIME .... MILEAGE END ....

ARRIVAL TIME .... MILEAGE TOTAL ....

CAMPSITE NAME ....

ADDRESS 1 ....

ADDRESS 2 ....

POST CODE .... GPS ....

E MAIL .... PHONE ....

WEBSITE WWW..

MY RATING ☆☆☆☆☆☆☆☆☆☆ RECOMMEND YES/NO

WHAT 3 WORDS LOCATION ....

NUMBER OF NIGHTS HERE ....

PEOPLE WE MET - NAMES, E MAIL, PHONE NUMBER

....

....

....

....

DAILY COSTS		TODAY'S HIGHLIGHTS
SITE FEES	£	....
FUEL	£	....
LPG GAS	£	....
TOLLS	£	....
GROCERIES	£	....
EATING OUT	£	....
ENTERTAINMENT	£	....
OTHER COSTS	£	....

NOTES

....

....

....

....

....

CAMPING TRAVEL JOURNAL

DATE ..../..../.........   MILEAGE START ....

START TIME ....   MILEAGE END ....

ARRIVAL TIME ....   MILEAGE TOTAL ....

CAMPSITE NAME ....

ADDRESS 1 ....

ADDRESS 2 ....

POST CODE ....   GPS ....

E MAIL ....   PHONE ....

WEBSITE WWW..

MY RATING ☆☆☆☆☆☆☆☆☆☆   RECOMMEND YES/NO

WHAT 3 WORDS LOCATION ....

NUMBER OF NIGHTS HERE ....

PEOPLE WE MET - NAMES, E MAIL, PHONE NUMBER

....

....

....

....

DAILY COSTS

SITE FEES	£	....
FUEL	£	....
LPG GAS	£	....
TOLLS	£	....
GROCERIES	£	....
EATING OUT	£	....
ENTERTAINMENT	£	....
OTHER COSTS	£	....

TODAY'S HIGHLIGHTS

....

....

....

....

....

....

....

NOTES

....

....

....

....

....

CAMPING TRAVEL JOURNAL

DATE ..../..../......... MILEAGE START ....

START TIME .... MILEAGE END ....

ARRIVAL TIME .... MILEAGE TOTAL ....

CAMPSITE NAME ....

ADDRESS 1 ....

ADDRESS 2 ....

POST CODE .... GPS ....

E MAIL .... PHONE ....

WEBSITE WWW..

MY RATING ☆☆☆☆☆☆☆☆☆☆ RECOMMEND YES/NO

WHAT 3 WORDS LOCATION ....

NUMBER OF NIGHTS HERE ....

PEOPLE WE MET - NAMES, E MAIL, PHONE NUMBER

....

....

....

....

DAILY COSTS		TODAY'S HIGHLIGHTS
SITE FEES	£	....
FUEL	£	....
LPG GAS	£	....
TOLLS	£	....
GROCERIES	£	....
EATING OUT	£	....
ENTERTAINMENT	£	....
OTHER COSTS	£	....

NOTES

....

....

....

....

....

CAMPING TRAVEL JOURNAL

DATE ..../..../........ MILEAGE START ....

START TIME .... MILEAGE END ....

ARRIVAL TIME .... MILEAGE TOTAL ....

CAMPSITE NAME ....

ADDRESS 1 ....

ADDRESS 2 ....

POST CODE .... GPS ....

E MAIL .... PHONE ....

WEBSITE WWW..

MY RATING ☆☆☆☆☆☆☆☆☆☆ RECOMMEND YES/NO

WHAT 3 WORDS LOCATION ....

NUMBER OF NIGHTS HERE ....

PEOPLE WE MET - NAMES, E MAIL, PHONE NUMBER

....
....
....
....

DAILY COSTS		TODAY'S HIGHLIGHTS
SITE FEES	£	....
FUEL	£	....
LPG GAS	£	....
TOLLS	£	....
GROCERIES	£	....
EATING OUT	£	....
ENTERTAINMENT	£	....
OTHER COSTS	£	....

NOTES

....
....
....
....
....

CAMPING TRAVEL JOURNAL

DATE ..../..../......... MILEAGE START ....

START TIME .... MILEAGE END ....

ARRIVAL TIME .... MILEAGE TOTAL ....

CAMPSITE NAME ....

ADDRESS 1 ....

ADDRESS 2 ....

POST CODE .... GPS ....

E MAIL .... PHONE ....

WEBSITE WWW..

MY RATING ☆☆☆☆☆☆☆☆☆☆ RECOMMEND YES/NO

WHAT 3 WORDS LOCATION ....

NUMBER OF NIGHTS HERE ....

PEOPLE WE MET - NAMES, E MAIL, PHONE NUMBER

....

....

....

....

DAILY COSTS		TODAY'S HIGHLIGHTS
SITE FEES	£	....
FUEL	£	....
LPG GAS	£	....
TOLLS	£	....
GROCERIES	£	....
EATING OUT	£	....
ENTERTAINMENT	£	....
OTHER COSTS	£	....

NOTES

....

....

....

....

....

CAMPING TRAVEL JOURNAL

DATE   ..../..../.........   MILEAGE START ....
START TIME ....   MILEAGE END   ....
ARRIVAL TIME ....   MILEAGE TOTAL ....

CAMPSITE NAME ....
ADDRESS 1 ....
ADDRESS 2 ....
POST CODE ....   GPS ....
E MAIL ....   PHONE ....
WEBSITE WWW...
MY RATING ☆☆☆☆☆☆☆☆☆☆   RECOMMEND YES/NO
WHAT 3 WORDS LOCATION ....
NUMBER OF NIGHTS HERE ....

PEOPLE WE MET - NAMES, E MAIL, PHONE NUMBER
....
....
....
....

DAILY COSTS		TODAY'S HIGHLIGHTS
SITE FEES	£	....
FUEL	£	....
LPG GAS	£	....
TOLLS	£	....
GROCERIES	£	....
EATING OUT	£	....
ENTERTAINMENT	£	....
OTHER COSTS	£	....

NOTES
....
....
....
....
....

CAMPING TRAVEL JOURNAL

DATE ..../..../......... MILEAGE START ....

START TIME .... MILEAGE END ....

ARRIVAL TIME .... MILEAGE TOTAL ....

CAMPSITE NAME ....

ADDRESS 1 ....

ADDRESS 2 ....

POST CODE .... GPS ....

E MAIL .... PHONE ....

WEBSITE WWW...

MY RATING ☆ ☆ ☆ ☆ ☆ ☆ ☆ ☆ ☆ ☆   RECOMMEND YES/NO

WHAT 3 WORDS LOCATION ....

NUMBER OF NIGHTS HERE ....

PEOPLE WE MET - NAMES, E MAIL, PHONE NUMBER

....
....
....
....

DAILY COSTS		TODAY'S HIGHLIGHTS
SITE FEES	£	....
FUEL	£	....
LPG GAS	£	....
TOLLS	£	....
GROCERIES	£	....
EATING OUT	£	....
ENTERTAINMENT	£	....
OTHER COSTS	£	....

NOTES

....
....
....
....
....

CAMPING TRAVEL JOURNAL

DATE   ..../..../.........   MILEAGE START ....

START TIME ....   MILEAGE END   ....

ARRIVAL TIME ....   MILEAGE TOTAL ....

CAMPSITE NAME ....

ADDRESS 1 ....

ADDRESS 2 ....

POST CODE ....   GPS ....

E MAIL ....   PHONE ....

WEBSITE WWW..

MY RATING ☆☆☆☆☆☆☆☆☆☆   RECOMMEND YES/NO

WHAT 3 WORDS LOCATION ....

NUMBER OF NIGHTS HERE ....

PEOPLE WE MET - NAMES, E MAIL, PHONE NUMBER

....

....

....

....

DAILY COSTS		TODAY'S HIGHLIGHTS
SITE FEES	£	....
FUEL	£	....
LPG GAS	£	....
TOLLS	£	....
GROCERIES	£	....
EATING OUT	£	....
ENTERTAINMENT	£	....
OTHER COSTS	£	....

NOTES

....

....

....

....

....

CAMPING TRAVEL JOURNAL

DATE ..../..../......... MILEAGE START ....

START TIME .... MILEAGE END ....

ARRIVAL TIME .... MILEAGE TOTAL ....

CAMPSITE NAME ....

ADDRESS 1 ....

ADDRESS 2 ....

POST CODE .... GPS ....

E MAIL .... PHONE ....

WEBSITE WWW..

MY RATING ☆☆☆☆☆☆☆☆☆☆ RECOMMEND YES/NO

WHAT 3 WORDS LOCATION ....

NUMBER OF NIGHTS HERE ....

PEOPLE WE MET - NAMES, E MAIL, PHONE NUMBER

....

....

....

....

DAILY COSTS		TODAY'S HIGHLIGHTS
SITE FEES	£	....
FUEL	£	....
LPG GAS	£	....
TOLLS	£	....
GROCERIES	£	....
EATING OUT	£	....
ENTERTAINMENT	£	....
OTHER COSTS	£	....

NOTES

....

....

....

....

....

CAMPING TRAVEL JOURNAL

DATE ..../..../......... MILEAGE START ....

START TIME .... MILEAGE END ....

ARRIVAL TIME .... MILEAGE TOTAL ....

CAMPSITE NAME ....

ADDRESS 1 ....

ADDRESS 2 ....

POST CODE .... GPS ....

E MAIL .... PHONE ....

WEBSITE WWW...

MY RATING ☆☆☆☆☆☆☆☆☆☆ RECOMMEND YES/NO

WHAT 3 WORDS LOCATION ....

NUMBER OF NIGHTS HERE ....

PEOPLE WE MET - NAMES, E MAIL, PHONE NUMBER

....
....
....
....

DAILY COSTS	TODAY'S HIGHLIGHTS
SITE FEES £	....
FUEL £	....
LPG GAS £	....
TOLLS £	....
GROCERIES £	....
EATING OUT £	....
ENTERTAINMENT £	....
OTHER COSTS £	....

NOTES

....
....
....
....
....

CAMPING TRAVEL JOURNAL

DATE ..../..../......... MILEAGE START ....

START TIME .... MILEAGE END ....

ARRIVAL TIME .... MILEAGE TOTAL ....

CAMPSITE NAME ....

ADDRESS 1 ....

ADDRESS 2 ....

POST CODE .... GPS ....

E MAIL .... PHONE ....

WEBSITE WWW..

MY RATING ☆☆☆☆☆☆☆☆☆☆ RECOMMEND YES/NO

WHAT 3 WORDS LOCATION ....

NUMBER OF NIGHTS HERE ....

PEOPLE WE MET - NAMES, E MAIL, PHONE NUMBER

....
....
....
....

DAILY COSTS		TODAY'S HIGHLIGHTS
SITE FEES	£	....
FUEL	£	....
LPG GAS	£	....
TOLLS	£	....
GROCERIES	£	....
EATING OUT	£	....
ENTERTAINMENT	£	....
OTHER COSTS	£	....

NOTES

....
....
....
....
....

CAMPING TRAVEL JOURNAL

DATE ..../..../......... MILEAGE START ....

START TIME .... MILEAGE END ....

ARRIVAL TIME .... MILEAGE TOTAL ....

CAMPSITE NAME ....

ADDRESS 1 ....

ADDRESS 2 ....

POST CODE .... GPS ....

E MAIL .... PHONE ....

WEBSITE WWW...

MY RATING ☆☆☆☆☆☆☆☆☆☆ RECOMMEND YES/NO

WHAT 3 WORDS LOCATION ....

NUMBER OF NIGHTS HERE ....

PEOPLE WE MET - NAMES, E MAIL, PHONE NUMBER

....
....
....
....

DAILY COSTS	TODAY'S HIGHLIGHTS
SITE FEES £	....
FUEL £	....
LPG GAS £	....
TOLLS £	....
GROCERIES £	....
EATING OUT £	....
ENTERTAINMENT £	....
OTHER COSTS £	....

NOTES

....
....
....
....
....

CAMPING TRAVEL JOURNAL

DATE ...../...../......... MILEAGE START ....

START TIME .... MILEAGE END ....

ARRIVAL TIME .... MILEAGE TOTAL ....

CAMPSITE NAME ....

ADDRESS 1 ....

ADDRESS 2 ....

POST CODE .... GPS ....

E MAIL .... PHONE ....

WEBSITE WWW...

MY RATING ☆☆☆☆☆☆☆☆☆☆ RECOMMEND YES/NO

WHAT 3 WORDS LOCATION ....

NUMBER OF NIGHTS HERE ....

PEOPLE WE MET - NAMES, E MAIL, PHONE NUMBER

....

....

....

....

DAILY COSTS		TODAY'S HIGHLIGHTS
SITE FEES	£	....
FUEL	£	....
LPG GAS	£	....
TOLLS	£	....
GROCERIES	£	....
EATING OUT	£	....
ENTERTAINMENT	£	....
OTHER COSTS	£	....

NOTES

....

....

....

....

....

CAMPING TRAVEL JOURNAL

DATE ..../..../......... MILEAGE START ....

START TIME .... MILEAGE END ....

ARRIVAL TIME .... MILEAGE TOTAL ....

CAMPSITE NAME ....

ADDRESS 1 ....

ADDRESS 2 ....

POST CODE .... GPS ....

E MAIL .... PHONE ....

WEBSITE WWW..

MY RATING ☆☆☆☆☆☆☆☆☆☆ RECOMMEND YES/NO

WHAT 3 WORDS LOCATION ....

NUMBER OF NIGHTS HERE ....

PEOPLE WE MET - NAMES, E MAIL, PHONE NUMBER

....

....

....

....

DAILY COSTS		TODAY'S HIGHLIGHTS
SITE FEES	£	....
FUEL	£	....
LPG GAS	£	....
TOLLS	£	....
GROCERIES	£	....
EATING OUT	£	....
ENTERTAINMENT	£	....
OTHER COSTS	£	....

NOTES

....

....

....

....

....

CAMPING TRAVEL JOURNAL

DATE ...../...../......... MILEAGE START ....
START TIME .... MILEAGE END ....
ARRIVAL TIME .... MILEAGE TOTAL ....

CAMPSITE NAME ....
ADDRESS I ....
ADDRESS 2 ....
POST CODE .... GPS ....
E MAIL .... PHONE ....
WEBSITE WWW...
MY RATING ☆☆☆☆☆☆☆☆☆☆ RECOMMEND YES/NO
WHAT 3 WORDS LOCATION ....
NUMBER OF NIGHTS HERE ....

PEOPLE WE MET - NAMES, E MAIL, PHONE NUMBER
....
....
....
....

DAILY COSTS		TODAY'S HIGHLIGHTS
SITE FEES	£	....
FUEL	£	....
LPG GAS	£	....
TOLLS	£	....
GROCERIES	£	....
EATING OUT	£	....
ENTERTAINMENT	£	....
OTHER COSTS	£	....

NOTES
....
....
....
....
....

Printed in Great Britain
by Amazon